Anonymous

Dublin Acrostics

Second Edition

Anonymous

Dublin Acrostics
Second Edition

ISBN/EAN: 9783337077358

Printed in Europe, USA, Canada, Australia, Japan

Cover: Foto ©ninafisch / pixelio.de

More available books at **www.hansebooks.com**

DUBLIN ACROSTICS.

"Like to a double cherry, seeming parted,
But yet a union in partition:
Two lovely berries moulded on one stem."

SECOND EDITION.

"There is, sure, another flood toward, and these couples are coming to the ark!"

DUBLIN:
HODGES, SMITH AND FOSTER.

1869.

PREFACE TO THE SECOND EDITION.

As the first Edition of the Dublin Acrostics has long been exhausted, and numerous enquiries have since been made for copies, a second Edition is now published. The first Edition has been revised, and fifty-six new Acrostics have been added. Those contained in the first Edition will be found in the present volume from 1 to 88 inclusive. The remainder are new.

PREFACE TO THE FIRST EDITION.

For the few who may possibly be yet unacquainted with the nature of a Double Acrostic, we give the following explanation. The initiated will skip it, and forgive us.

The Double Acrostic is a riddle, the answer to which is to be found in two words of an equal number of letters. The first portion of the riddle points to the words themselves, which form the answer: the second portion (to which numbers are prefixed) points to certain other words, the initial and final letters of which form respectively the two principal words. Hence the name of Double Acrostic. These words are termed "lights."

For example, take these lines from Swift:—

> I am jet black, as you may see,
>   The son of pitch and gloomy night,
> Yet all that know me will agree,
>   I'm dead except I live in light.
>
> Most wondrous is my magic power;
>   For, with one colour I can paint,—
> I'll make the devil a saint this hour,
>   Next, make a devil of a saint.
>
> Through distant regions I can fly,
>   Provide me with but paper wings;
> And fairly show a reason why
>   There should be quarrels among kings, &c.
>
> In youth, exalted high in air,
>   Or bathing in the waters fair,-

Nature to form me took delight,
And clad my body all in white.
My person tall, and slender waist,
On either sides with fringes graced;
Till me that tyrant, man, espied,
And dragged me from my mother's side.
My skin he flayed, my hair he cropped,
At head and foot my body lopped,
And then, with heart more hard than stone,
He picked my marrow from the bone.
To vex me more, he took a freak
To split my tongue and make me speak;
But that which wonderful appears,
I speak to eyes and not to ears, &c.

Now, if Swift had added verses (which we are far from venturing to add for him), indicating, with a due degree of ingenious obscurity, the following:—

1. A little devil.
2. The organ of smell.
3. The cooking apartment.

there would have been a complete Double Acrostic, the principal words being *ink* and *pen*, and the lights being,

    1. I m P.
    2. N o s E.
    3. Kitche N.

The two principal words may either be, as in the above instance, distinct words, having, however, some essential or accidental connexion, or else two words forming together a compound word, as in the ordinary charade. Whenever, in the following Double Acrostics, the Roman numerals I., II., III. are found, the numeral III. refers to the *whole*.

DUBLIN ACROSTICS.

No. 1.

SEARCH for my first the azure depths of heaven,
  The wreaths of harebell and forget-me-not,
Or the dear eyes of one whose love is given
  To smile upon thy home, and bless thy lot.
Search for my second in the hands of men,
  Those rigid types of rule, and strongly bound,
Yet giving worlds of thought to tongue and pen,
  In realms where boundless liberty is found.
But lo ! my first and second joined in one—
  Armstrong and Whitworth cannot reach its skill ;
Though vast the weight of each inventor's gun,
  Yet these reports shall live when theirs is still ;
For speech may falter, oaths may pass away,
  Divisions rend each human resolution,
Yet though our members perish day by day,
  Each noble act outlives a dissolution.

1. Oh! give me but a bit, and I am yours,
   Though far away from my own native moors.
2. A prison-house, I cannot tell you where,
   'Tis not in middle earth, or heaven, or air.
3. Once was I known the famous home of mysteries,
   Before Miss Braddon wrote her thrilling histories.
4. The Northern hunter's horn, a cheerful sign!
   But I will give him back no horn of mine.

           B.

No. 2.

I.

Double my first conveys what just will do.

II.

My second bears surprise from me to you.

III.

Only one voice hath ever sung me true.

  1. In pit profound.
  2. "Her swamps around,"

           R.

No 3.

I.

I slow and laborious,
Triumphant and glorious,
The **same,** ever-varying, trundle along,
Now through a multitude,
Now through a solitude,
Theme of a Pæan, a Dirge, **and a** Song.

II.

I fond and capricious,
Oft ugly and vicious,
Am loved by the worldling, the maiden, **the sage**:
Though praised by affection
As nearly perfection,
I stamp in a passion, or bark in a rage.

III.

Mock warriors **furious,**
And tales of the curious
By coming **to me are** endowed with renown.
Both small dissipation,
And less information
Are brought upon me **for the use of the town.**

1. A fish out of water, of slander a name.
2. My fate is a cloud on a hero's fair fame.
3. The Rifleman's miss, but the Engineer's aim.

           F.

No. 4.

Though not o'er Alpine snow and ice,
 But homely English ground,
"Excelsior" was our device,
 And sad the fate we found.
We did not climb from love of fame,
 But followed duty's call,
United were we in our aim,
 Though parted in our fall.

1. I am the crown of Irish mirth.
2. A Poet, or his place of birth.
3. A pretty toy, a hidden snare,
4. Fatal to me and all I bear.

           O.

No. 5.

When long ago **I** said my prayers,
    An infant, at my mother's knee,
If temper **I** displayed, **or airs**,
    She with **my first** admonished me.
At school when I and other boys
    With popguns gave the **birds a fright**,
And gaily laughed to **hear the noise**,
    My second was our prime delight.
But now a swell, I have **a soul**
    Above both first and second **raised**,
And oft I loudly cry my whole,
    Whilst sober people think **me crazed**.

1. This prefix marks inferiority.
2. **My** tenants hailed my coming home with glee.
3. **I look for** franchise to the Parliament.
4. **In** Ireland **I'm the** boy that pays the rent.

                                                H.

No. 6.

My first—a pretty girl—
    My second loves alway,
Although her brain it whirl,
    And lead her steps astray.

1. Such will angelic visits be.
2. Could Pen prefer pert Blanche to thee?
3. The time between the cup and lip.
4. Ah me! Nepenthe let me sip!
5. O precious jewel, amber bright!
   O " reverend and exquisite!"

O'B.

No. 7.

I.

Not pitch, though tossed.

II.

Hoof's sound is lost.

III.

I'm ever crossed.

1. How brays my blast!
2. A maiden fast.
3. Poor Rembrant's last.

R.

No. 8.

A god thou wert, and nations bowed
In silent awe and worship loud
To thee my first, and at thy feast
The naked sacrificial priest
In wild procession swept along,
With cymbals' clash, and rhythmic song.
These vain unhallowed rites are o'er,
Yet votaries still almost adore,
And eager myriads greet the hour
They feel thy vivifying power.
My all hath many a deep recess
Where treasures lie in uselessness,
Until thy glowing circle warms
Their plastic elemental forms.
My second is a spell-word known
To all who scale achievement's throne.
That monosyllable is fraught
With all the wisdom Bacon taught.

1. I am of all improvidence the goal.
2. Can I the page of destiny unroll?
3. Or wizard spell evoke the parted soul?

O.

No. 9.

The knight rides on in armour dight,
    His casque at saddle-bow,
The steed returns, but not the knight,
    My first has laid him low.
I ride the stream, all gaily clad,
    With plumes and silken garb,
And bear, though seeming light and glad,
    Sure death upon my barb.

1. The cottier loves my piping lay.
2. The tawny Hindoo's dye.
3. Of fickle love and counted gay.
4. Bad play's apology.   T.

No. 10.

Blest be the woodland way,
    And the well which the alders hide,
And the steed which I reined that day
    To drink in the warm noontide.
My steed, he drank of the well,
    But a dearer draught was mine;
'Twas my second bestowed the spell
    That flushed in my veins like wine.

Though my first, in those days as now,
  Belonged to my practised tongue,
Yet there the unspoken vow
  In formless accents hung.
But oft as again we stole
  To meetings more fond and free,
The first far glimpse of my whole
  Was fever and trance to me.

    1. A gushing thing.
    2. I close a spring.
    3. Admire my wing.

                         O.

No. 11.

High-mettled ride we! yet we show 'tis true
The triumph of the most successful screw.

1. To find my first, go seek the realm of letters.
2. Then seek the home of pleasure's rosy fetters.
3. The mournful requiem of a wounded bride.
4. The finless creatures of the foaming tide.

                         B.

No. 12.

Where Ethiopia's banjo
   A British audience cheers,
With waistcoat white, and riddle trite,
   Behold! my first appears.
But join my first and second—
   In rustic lane and field—
A cherished prize in boyhood's eyes
   My first and second yield.

1. Oh! splendid friend, though nicknamed by the low,
   Be ever friend of mine in weal or woe.
2. The moon shines bright, a maid from me descends,
   And with an unknown lover leaves her friends.
3. The gold received for me the Jew retains,
   Nor gives the squire a zecchin for his pains.
4. I trust I shan't my lady readers vex,
   But one has said I'm seldom in your sex.
5. Yon massy portal that obstructs your course,
   Flies open for me though I use no force.

R.

No. 13.

I.

An article of little worth, but still
On some occasions indispensable.

II.

Without my help stern Marmion's dying cheer
Had never reached his charging comrade's ear.

III.

Of old, at call of well-known name,
   I sprang responsive forth,
Now when I see the light, it is
   To hide some name of worth.

   1. 'Mid olives grey I gently steal along.
   2. A vot'ress I of wild romance and song.

M'D.

No. 14.

Two little words of letters three
    Comprising much in narrow span,
If taken singly let you see
    The direst rage of beast and man.
Reverse the first—you want a fire !
    Reverse the last—you see a name
Of one among the sable choir
    Whose head and harp have won him fame.
Unite the two, and forth to view
    An ancient title next will stand,
When Norman conquest still was new,
    The foremost champion of the land.
Now from the whole remove the head,
    You wander in a noble wood—
But hush ! for where you rashly tread,
    Creations of the poet stood.
Last from the whole strike off the tail,
    And Bramah's labours meet your eyes,
But chubby youth and captive wail
    Must also from the word arise.

1. Whether I should a table turn out or a god,
    Stood the classical joiner in doubt,
   And though times are so changed, still, admit it
    is odd,
    I a statesman or block may turn out.
2. Before me fall sovereigns, commoners, all,
    Though at times to the meanest I yield.
3. The fashions have altered since, slender and small,
    I was formed for the Dandy to wield.

F.

No. 15.

I.

Gem from her finger fell—
  Gift of her lover—
Long though she search and well,
  Ne'er to recover!

II.

Fast flow the maiden's tears—
  My hand can dry them—
Soothings to calm her fears?
  I can supply them.

III.

Fast as the waters slide
    Down in the river,
So from her bosom glide
    Jewel and giver.
Maiden, another's bride—
    Lover left rueing,
" Only my whole," he cried,
    " All my fond wooing !"

1. "They're off!" "Oh! are they?" lisps the languid swell,
He means the horses, I the legs as well.
2. This word in that command you're sure to find
Where Dante talks of leaving hope behind.
3. The fishers three would now be safe and sound,
If, far from me, they'd stayed upon dry ground.
4. Seek for me now in Erin's humblest home,
Though once my wit delighted ancient Rome.

R.

No. 16.

Whether **in prose or** gentle verse, 'tis plain
An adjective unyielding I remain;
When joined **to** ship of whatsoever fleet
I **trust** the reader **me** may never meet.

A source of good **and evil to mankind**,
What many seek for, but what **few can find**,
Of which but few can learn good use **to make**,
And aid **their fellows for their fellows' sake.**

1. Where'er it comes, a wildly mournful **strain**,
   And dire confusion, hate, and terror reign.
2. **The** tuneful Darky comes **from** distant me,
   Love in his heart and **banjo on** his knee.
3. **In intervals like** this our Solons turn
   Their thoughts and energies **to fresh** intent,
   In order that, invigorate, **they may earn**
   Their **country's** praise, their own emolument.
4. Rapid my pious exercises are,
   No Christianity more **muscular** !

O'C.

No. 17.

I.

In deserts wild I savage-clad appear—
To guide a stately fleet I'd volunteer—
My sightless eye-balls yearn for " Holy Light "—
I gained my fame by visions of the night.

II.

I bleed and die amid unpitying cheers—
Where I am uttered I'm received with jeers—
With bears I grapple in perpetual war—
My virgin burden I conveyed afar.

III.

I hate the Yankee, I despise " Mossoo,"
I loathe the Dutchman, and the Russian too,
I laugh at Paddy, Sawny hold in scorn,
For I to rule the Universe was born.

1. What Whigs and Tories both alike enjoy.
2. Treasure like gold, but not without alloy.
3. The home of misery I oft am found.
4. In Yankee speech I am the common sound.

H.

No. 18.

Of common birth, of elements the same,
The first with more of fire and firmer frame
Protects, until a common doom they share,
The second, of a mould more soft and fair.

1. **If** measured, you will **always trace**
   From rim to rim an equal **space.**
2. The famous sage, it **must** be **owned,**
   Produced a famous vagabond.
3. Than wildest Nænia **wilder still,**
   The **Irish** cry is **on** the **hill.**
4. The brain-sick youth hath startled **all**
   The revellers **in** that northern hall.
5. **Your " bookish theoric" 's a** fool,
   'Tis **I** afford the safest **rule.**

O.

No. 19.

My first a traveller, and " one of three,"
Though stout, yet like " the ribbed sea sand " was he.
Sad Jaques found my second in the woods,
And both express his contemplative moods.

      1. Encore !
      2. Deplore !
      3. French ore.
      5. Fresh gore.
      5. New lore.

                        K.

No. 20.

Two beings in mid-air at times
Were found in far removèd climes.
See one on high, like lightning flash,
Dart at the Pole with sudden dash,
The other painfully and slow
Along the Line move to and fro !

1. The fount of nature's songsters' sweetest strains.
2. The silent record of a man's **demise.**
3. **A river** wandering over sun-lit plains.
4. A time refreshing to the weary **eyes.**
5. The careful guardian of a maiden's fame.
6. A carping cynic's cruel cutting tooth.
7. A youthful Edward's once familiar name.
    Soothsayers say! Where lies the hidden sooth?

F.

No. 21.

To have me robbed a jovial **rouè cried,**
Who deeply drank, and just as deeply lied.
To keep me full—a task found ofttimes vain—
The **rival** party-chieftains fiercely strain.

By big-wigged **Doctors scorned, and** overthrown,
By cotton Lords I'm fostered as their **own.**
I'm quick to calculate, **I'm apt to speak**—
I think in figures, and **I** dream **in Greek.**

1. Brightest of **jewels, most** resplendent,
   From blackest **negro I am** pendent.

2. If Ali Baba had a Roman been,
    This number on his corps you would have seen.
3. Ills I foretold; but men withheld belief,
    And for their scorning often came to grief.
4. Two armies met, and charged in mortal strife,
    They changed a dynasty, I lost my life.
5. Where sunny Isles lie scattered on the Sea,
    Each maid's heart fluttered as she thought of me.
6. "I bet five pounds upon it!" "Done! you win,"
    Again.   "Now, sir, you lose; I save my tin."
7. A grim old castle, ghosts, a rattling chain,
    Mysterious sounds with awful shrieks of pain.
8. Free me, Ye Powers, from Fenian plots I pray,
    And Yankee filibusters keep away!
9. In this fierce contest, and at Epsom too,
    Was well avenged the fight of Waterloo.

H.

No. 22.

A lawless, robbing, wandering life hath led
  My second—but I quote a daft Divine.
Like Omphale with Hercules, light thread
  Leads my strong first—I crown the custard fine.

1. I follow on the frolics of the knight.
2. The bar can ne'er forget my noble light.
3. Poetasters me both last, and least indite.

K.

No. 23.

DOUBLE DOUBLE ACROSTIC.

Let poets praise the daughters of the sea,
Why should her sons unsung, unhonoured be?

A.

1.

My teeth are strong, you guard your trunks in vain,
I can destroy them, though against the grain.

2.

The history student knows my name full well,
And through my land's divisions this will tell.

3.

Monarch and slave, the blesséd and the cursed,
The noblest of all creatures, and the worst.

4.

"I know a bank whereon the wild thyme grows,"
But many a bank my time and treasure knows.

5.

That which the poor can seldom taste, but which
Flies also the caprices of the rich.

6.

Broken by you, yet still our sport the same,
I share the toil, that you may win the game.

B.

1.

A place of rest, where parties don't run high,
No foe to truth—it helps mankind to lie.

2.

One great experience this great **name** discloses,
A bed **of** gold is not a bed **of** roses.

3.

As down parade **in time the** soldiers pace,
Full oft they hear **me round each** veteran's face.

4.

Go, search the winning gambler's desk, **and look**
What debts of honour **no** evasion brook.

5.

This word gave rise to many a Papal tussle :
If still it lives **I** know not, ask Lord Russell.

6.

The hero stands the charge unmoved, **we** know ; -
But give **me one** small charge, and off I go.

B.

No. 24. 1st Oct., 1865.

Two well-known words be mine the task to sing,
Two, yet expressive of a single thing,
Whose form, though every where 'tis ours to scan,
Though bought and sold, is never used by man.
Of girls' capriciousness it yields a proof
They love it more the more it keeps aloof,
What varied chance its strange existence meets!
It flaunts at court, it humbly sweeps the streets.
Of agonizing death too oft the cause,
Yet irrepressible by any laws;
Abused, derided, still it holds its sway,
How long 'twill do so, who can dare to say?*

1. What once a hero scorned to bow before.
2. The tedious twaddle of a humdrum bore.
3. I'm neither he nor she, with both though blent.
4. What reigned on earth ere Lucifer was sent.
5. A victim of the terrible Lucrece.
6. An adjective we borrow from great Greece.
7. An earthly Queen to Olympian honours brought.
8. A glory of great waters grandly fraught.
9. An honest representative of aught.   K.

* How long indeed! 1869.

No. 25.

Two graceful beings born in different ages—
  The younger—maid of gay and sportive **mien**—
Of fancies strange—whilst she in play engages
  She wields **a club,** and shuns all crinoline;
Yet hoops she loves, nor cares for balls without them,
  And as for colors—why she raves about them!
The elder—full of strength aud manly grace—
  And, though on noble field-pursuits **intent,**
Ofttimes a ball he joyfully will face,
  His **eyes** upon his partner's closely **bent;**
Fond of **a** catch, and reading from the **score,**
  Though thinking "going out" an awful bore.

1. Old Republican! thine honours were in honesty laid down,
    Thou didst **scorn to** seize **by** violence **or** perfidy a crown.
2. Where **Atlas** mountains through **the clouds do** peep.
    I oft disturb **the** wearied traveller's sleep.
3. When the Christian warriors bravely sought **to** lay proud Russia low,
    Started from our slumbers **we** too helped **to strike** the gallant **blow.**

4. In Spain I've gained a deathless fame, ⎫
   Oft daring deeds go by my name ⎬
   To which, too, rashness lays a claim. ⎭
5. Lovely stream, whose beauties ofttimes have the bardic legends sung,
   And whose shores have erst with laughter of high lords and ladies rung!
6. Fair maid, with name expressive of thy purity and truth,
   How hopeless the pursuit of the fond love of thy youth!
7. Imperial Rome is in a blaze—
   Her Emperor his fiddle plays.

H.

No. 26.

Severed, we summon to action,
Blent, we're an obsolete fraction.

1. Seat of successive empires lost and won.
2. Seat of that seat, proud region of the sun.

O.

No. 27.

Now, like a ruthless despot
  Whom trembling crowds obey,
My first subdues and crushes
  All things beneath its sway.
A noted bruiser also—
  And greater than Jem Mace—
For Mace beneath its counters
  Would be in evil case.
But hark! (and small the change is)
  The Magyar captive brave
By funeral chimes, low pealing,
  Is summoned to his grave.
To deal forth death and ruin,
  To scatter and destroy,
And cause the worst disunion
  Is oft my second's joy.
And yet—oh! seeming marvel—
  As oft its chief delight
With soft and gentle influence
  To strengthen and unite.
But when my first and second
  Their agency combine,

(As quickened by affliction,
    The truest virtues shine)
So crushed, oppressed, but bettered
    By their most cruel test,
The power that erst slept uselessly
    Brings peace, and joy, and rest.

1. Ah! cruel chimes, ye sound love's funeral knell—
    The sailor bids his weeping maid farewell.
2. Time, and life's ordeal, alone can show
    If true or false the metal be below.
3. Give me my friend, with him, oh! wealth untold
    Of gleaming jewels, and of ruddy gold.
4. Poor Mantalini! for thy wife no more
    Consents to liquidate thy little score.
5. Even as we seek for violets in the shade,
    So did thy lover seek thee, gentle maid!
6. Down from the hill the young Ascanius came
    Panting for nobler foe—more dangerous game.

R.

No. 28.

Fleeting, fierce, of brief endurance,
We're united in assurance.

1. Loud and joyous is the chorus!
2. Opera goers all adore us.
3. Steady boys! there's death before us.
4. I describe the power of **Porus**.   F.

No. 29.

In the first, when reversed,
Many heroes were nursed,
Who **filled the** whole world with their fame.
The second's accursed,
'Tis surely the worst
Of all sources of sorrow and shame.
The fetters now burst
The multitude durst
Its inherited liberty claim.

1. Emblems of pain.
2. Slaying and slain.
3. Certainly plain.   F.

No. 30.

My first's a source of bitter strife
  'Twixt giver and receiver.
My second's that of which alone
  Dare drink the true believer.

1. Fashioned by toil of man and beast.
2. What courtiers almost live in.
3. With post combined, by cravens shunned.
4. More taken far than given.   T.

No. 31.

The steed comes forth—the armour's clasped—
  A lady, lily-fair,
(My second to her bosom grasped)
  Speeds down the turret-stair.
"Oh! wear it"—and from out her breast
  A token white she draws—
"Oh! wear it, 'tis my own behest,
  For me, and for the cause."
He bent him from the champing Roan,
  And clasped the pale ladye,
"So sweet, so white, like you my own,
  This token seems to me."

White upturned face of tearful bride
    He nearer—nearer **drew,**
"**I'll wear it** for the cause," he cried,
    "**And kiss it, sweet! for you.**"
That champing Roan the far-off fight
    Or knows, or seems to know,
With eye on fire, and crest dashed white,
    As torrent **flecked** with snow.
The knight the needless rowel drove,
    He dared not turn or **pause,**
"I'll live to love my **own true** love,
    Or die for my loved cause."
But lo! of kingly cavaliers
    Out flaunts the banner-blaze,
Proud Percies, Hollands, Staffords, **Veres,**
    And turbulent Courtneys!
The ring of onset **rends** the sky,
    No courser idly paws,
Ah! hark! that loyal battle-cry,
    "One only **love,** one cause!"

    *   *   *   *   *

She parts upon his pallid brow
    The locks his heart hath dyed:

All marble-wan, and tearless now,
   The woe-stunned widowed bride;
For, smitten down in fiercest strife
   By foreman's whirling blade,
He lost together love and life
   My baffled first to aid.
Ah! why should things that never move
   Forsake a losing side?
His heart beat true to chief and love,
   Till ceased to throb its tide.
But stark·in death the badge he bore
   Proved false to his behest,
For type of alien cause he wore
   Upon his gory breast.

1. Two-worded I, to-day's equivalent
   To what poor Frank's " Anon, anon, Sir," meant.
2. When dies the blossom drooping from the tree,
   I keep for ever sweet her memory.
3. A man of mine a bard hath nobly sung,
   And told how lisped his name each infant tongue.
4. "So dear, so dear" the Miller's daughter grew,
   Oh dear! how dear poor pestered we've grown too!

K.

No. 32.

I.

I am one-half of Europe's proudest city—
I am a lord more pompous far than witty—
In colleges I exercise control—
O'er frozen plains my icy billows roll.

II.

Poor Mistress Bluebeard sat disconsolate
Talking to sister Anne about her fate,
And said, whilst asking if she saw relief,
I was the cause of all her cares and grief.

III.

Whilst deeds of chivalry entranced the knight,
I was the squire's dear solace and delight—
And one far-famed in noted comedy
Once said he wished himself set down for me.

1. One source from whence come England's future kings.
2. I am alone, to me no comrade clings.
3. Whene'er a mighty hero asks for fame,
   Humanity shall thunder out my name.

H.

No. 33.

Whispering of peace, yet hostile to repose,
I give divided joys, divided woes.

My common attribute is shame,
And yet, when from my first I spring,
I'm often linked with honour's name,
And draw my being from a king.

1. When you say me, no worse remains to say.
2. What every lover loves, that peerless wonder!
3. What when you've solved me you'll exclaim to-day.
4. What marks the author's not the printer's blunder.
5. The plunderer once but now the prey of plunder.

O.

No. 34.

In happy **ball,** 'mid music's swell,
The darlings **of each** bright-eyed belle,
    My first and second see,
No valse complete **without the** twain—
Without my first e'en Godfrey's strain
    Were vapid melody.
Though both are wont to galop well,
Yet gallop, yet spelt with double **L,**
    My first alone employs.
Though staffs with both **are** often graced,
My second, ever highest placed,
    The top alone enjoys.

1. My slighted love at last with joy was crowned.
2. My Queen was given to love both bank and brae.
3. With monarch proud **my name** in lay renowned.
4. A city placed upon a famous **bay.**
5. Buried by anxious parent in the ground.
6. Me Angelina cried at close of day.

                        K. & R.

No. 35.

The secrets to my second told
My first too often doth unfold.
    1. Never true.
    2. Not always new.
    3. Always two.   O'B.

No. 36.

I.

Whenever me a singer sings,
    The tone so sadly falls
That, lo! an obvious shudder thrills
    The crescent of the stalls.

II.

I clothe some monsters of the deep—
    Men named a chief from me—
Me ever wore the nameless one—
    In me a cycle see.

III.

As nature sleeps beneath the snow
    Which icy winter left,
So sleeps my whole by cold o'ercome,
    Of all its powers bereft.

But still as nature buds again
    Beneath spring's quickening beams,
So warmth invigorates my whole
    And smooths what crumpled seems.

1. Though Bright with democratic tongue
    May strive to raise a storm,
  England, I ween, can ne'er forget
    My efforts for Reform.
2. The passing bell is echoing
    Through Magdalen's vaulted aisle,
  While eager crowds around me throng
    Laid on my funeral pile.
3. As maids and youths in mazy dance
    Sported on summer days,
  Ferrara's halls oft echoed with
    My songs and roundelays.
4. I have with glowing beauty decked
    The Adriatic's queen,
  Proud dames and haughty senators
    Have oft my subjects been.

                    T.

No. 37.

When my first is arrived at a shout loud and clear
  Will peal up from the friends of Will Gladstone the caustic,
And none for the kingdom my second shall fear,
  Though its name you may give to this double acrostic;
While my whole jabbers on what he's taught to express,
Like a member reciting his maiden address.

  1. I lived through many and many a year.
  2. I swept the skies with studious eyes,
  3. Nor dreamt of what's to weary minds so dear.

W.

No. 38.

Thus he said, but said it *sotto*
  Voce, (for he feared mamma),
"I have taken for my motto,
  Glissez mais n'appuyez pas."

Pleasant **transitory** fancies,
　　Pic-nic, Croquet, Boat and Ball,
Interchange of hands and glances,
　　Lips, perhaps—but that is all.
So his heart against the charmer
　　Deemed itself securely steeled,
Such resolves are feeble armour
　　When our fate is in the field.
Need I tell you how it ended?
　　How the fish was brought aground;
'Twas my first that he intended,
　　'Twas my second that he found.

1. Shriek! **I didn't; no one** heard it,
　　Though a rhyming Scot averred it.
2. Home from carnage on the water
　　For a little private slaughter.
3. I've forgotten Wordsworth's **poem**,
　　'Tis from Walter Scott **I** know him.
4. I suspect that Hebrews covet,
　　And I know that Christians love **it.**
5. Water in a trifling hurry,
　　Foam and Iris—Byron—Murray.

6. If he left her for another,
   Pray does that make me her mother?
7. Not a hunter, nor a racer,
   What I want's a steady pacer.
8. On a two-fold board I flourish,
   Now I smooth, and now I nourish.   o.

No. 39.

I.

I rang along the serried line,
When rode to war the Geraldine.

II.

A well-known proverb prays that I
May rest in lone tranquillity.

III.

I rank with kings—though plain my state
Than I what monarch e'er more great?

1. The poet sings my heavenly leap,
2. In dear old nursery me.
3. I doze my days in ivied keep.
4. Not made, though brewed should be.

K.

No. 40.

I.

A bishop once my virtues loudly praised,
For which his brother bishops called him **crazed**,
But still my qualities are far from mean,
For though I'm dirty, **I keep others** clean.

II.

When through the fleet the **magic** signal **ran**
That England hoped **for aid from every man**,
I heard those words **with inspiration** fraught,
And with **our** glorious Nelson **bravely** fought.

III.

In deserts wild I lead a nomad life,
And to my neighbours am a source of strife.
But if to bag your game you stretch your net,
In me a prey most troublesome you get.

1. I scattered o'er the raging main
2. The fleet that once sailed forth from Spain.
3. **And I,** the few that did remain,
4. Assisted to their homes again.

H.

No 41.

Robber and thief in ancient Rome,
What now we always see at home
    With otter, hare, or ermine.
What used in snow and wintry sleet,
Catarrh and asthma will defeat,
    I leave you to determine.

1. Old-fashioned watch and chain in me.
2. Ever a man in Italy.
3. A rose diminutive you see.

No. 42.

I served the palmer's humble needs,
    I served the hermit in his cell,
My comrades were the staff and beads,
    The sandal shoon and scallop-shell.
Alas! the worst corruption springs,
'Tis written, from the purest things.
Companion now of all that's base,
    The servant of a knavish crew,
To me his fall the dupe may trace,
    To me his rise the parvenu.

And yet, whatever be asserted,
My hope is still to be converted.

Insensible, and **dull**, and **hard** !
   Are these **the names** to me you give ?
Not aspen-leaf, not seaman's card,
   More tremulous and sensitive,
By turns elated **and** depressed,
   With every breath **from east or** west.
Though now you scarce can recognize
   My yoke upon the necks of men,
Though flung aside for looser ties,
   Yet am I not—I ask again—
The proudest **boast** of lineage high ?
What numbers wish my first were I.

   1. Brightly shone the sinuous gold,
   2. When to **me the** mayor **was wending**.
   3. Love that sprang from hate **of old**.
   4. For my captive daughter **bending**.
   5. Merry, mischievous, **and** bold.

                                              O.

No. 43.

I.

Within the compass of each madman's head,
I too go mad, when winter snows are fled.

II.

Sweet, sad, and merry, harsh, and loud, and low,
Instinct with feeling to the heart I go.

III.

With head low bowed while howls the blast in vain,
I wait in hope till sunshine come again.

    1. The best place in winter to cower.
    2. A quadrisyllabic flower.
    3. The certain result of a shower.
    4. What defies even time's fatal power.

M'D.

No. 44.

A noble race and puny line
In me mysteriously combine.
A puny line and little noted,
Although above all others voted.
Men dub me great, and, vastly prized,
In every creed I'm canonized.

They're gleaming up the far-off hill,
Fond hopes—blank fears—the concourse thrill.
Down sweeps tumultuous and compact,
The variegated cataract!
Loud hopes—shrill fears—together soar
Upon the May breeze—all is o'er.

1. They cast me off the lowest depths who seek.
2. Me Sunday gives mechanics once a week.
3. A hero I, of thrilling lordly rhyme,
4. When taken at the flood then comes my time,
5. O More I crave, then name a cheerful chime.

K.

No. 45.

I.

Of ribald populace the royal sport—
At home, abroad, I kept a jovial court—
The patron saint I am of every whig—
And once I wrote most pleasantly of pig.

II.

A phrase genteel when speaking of the devil—
A nickname for that potent prince of evil—
That name a merry wife did once invoke
When of her " pretty weathercock" she spoke.

III.

A monthly gift I gave for many years,
Received with laughter now, and now with tears.
Those gifts once welcome, now so rarely seen,
Still sometimes serve to keep my mem'ry green.

1. I was bedecked in comical arrray
    When donkeys from the grass were driven away.

2. When in his chambers he received his guest
   'Twas thus the chancellor his pet addressed.
3. On this he braved the fury of the gale
   To gather notes and to adorn a tale.
4. Foregoing all the joys of home and love
   In search of phantoms wearily he strove.
5. I was his friend in all his cares and strife,
   He bought my skin, and yet he spared my life.
6. He sought a home, far, far beyond the sea.
   And nearly fainted when he gazed on me.
7. Loathsome in person, and debased in mind,
   His soul to cruelty and fraud inclined!

L'Envoi.

Go, search my whole with anxious care,
And all my parts discover there.

No. 46.

The Norman Baron from the cowering Jew
Would wring his wealth by tortures not a few,
And yet you'll shudder when you hear me say
I go through tortures quite as bad each day.
I'm cut and hacked, and then, oh! torment dire,
I'm slowly roasted at a red-hot fire.
And lest this malice one device should lack,
I'm often after placed upon the rack.
And yet I'm guiltless, though, my woes to crown,
By any fool I'm easily done brown.

The second take, and, by the aid of fire,
See! quickly springs to life, at man's desire,
A mighty instrument of giant force,
In power resistless, boundless in resource.
'Tis sometimes bright and clear as morning light,
'Tis sometimes dark and drear as wintry night.
Uncertain you may find it, hard or soft,
Now in the earth, now in the clouds aloft,
You often see it both in joy and woe,
If others' joys and others' griefs you know.

My first and second joined **demand scant praise**,
Nor are they worthy of the poet's **lays**,
At them and at their friends **let's hurl defiance**,
And leave them to the Temperance Alliance!

1. The snows are fled, th**e** ice has passed away,
   Verdure **once more appears** beneath my sway.
2. Four great divisions of **the** world pass by,
   A fifth remains, and lo! that fifth am I.
3. The lonely wife in that dread, **fatal** hour,
   Made use of me to foil the beldame's **power**.
4. Nor love can fail, nor friends away **can flee**,
   If such your love and such your friendship **be**.
5. 'Tis said, however wounding to my vanity,
   I'm but a feeble fraction of humanity.

R.

No. 47.

From abstract riddles riddled all,
    I turn, despairing, to concrete.
My first alone disjointed fall,
    And all the owner's plans defeat.

My second too, a shapeless thing
    Hath by itself been riddled oft.
Let each to other firmly cling,
    And both together rise aloft.

1. Home of the angel of industry bright.
2. Regions rebellious without us.
3. I, whilst this idle acrostic I write.
4. A circle at length drawn about us.
5. All silently marking the statesman's address.
6. Nor waves can appal me, nor tempests oppress.

F.

No. 48.

I.

I guarded once old England's sea-girt shore—
I to a monarch's spirit panic bore—
To lash a grievance once I served a Dean—
No brilliant landscape without me is seen.

II.

Without my aid your beer would cease to flow—
In me the British lion hath a foe—
I tended infancy with anxious care—
I sometimes show the currents of the air.

III.

From foreign climes a welcome guest I come.
And make the wildest solitude my home.
I in patrician banquets rule the roast,
And there am sure to be the favourite toast.

1. If on your letters you direct to me,
   You're sure to find a judge or a Q.C.
2. If for a wholesome diet you're inclined,
   No doubt in me you get one to your mind.
3. Your limbs rheumatic, if they aching be,
   Are greatly soothed by rubbing them with me.

4. For benefit of passengers and trade,
   Let sea-bound vessels be in me surveyed.

               H.

No. 49.

I.
No lingering sparks about the wick remain.
II.
Who would be I, 'mid whistling wind and rain?
III.
A strong superlative the linkèd twain.

1. A well known Russell ever follows me.
2. In these twin letters yet another see.
3. I perch, and pipe, and flit from tree to tree.

            K.

No. 50.

The weaver weaves his woof in hope,
 The spinner spins from day to day,
Though far beyond his little scope
 His varied work must court display.
Gay beauty flaunts the glittering prize,
While cold and stiff the maker lies.

Aye—gaily on from **flower** to flower
  The thoughtless insect **fluttering goes,**
She sports, the darling of the hour,
  Bows to the lily, courts the rose,
Yet lives the emblem of the blest
And finds her home on Psyche's crest.

1. I come when I'm **called and I go where I'm** bid.
2. See! where **the cook found the sandwiches hid.**
3. Change **sides—ye are still Hanoverian vermin.**
4. Fair sail—only pleasure **your cruise may determine.**
5. Welcome **sight to the sailor on tempest-tossed sea.**
6. **Now tuneful, now** mute, **we live** only **in thee.**
7. I'm the staff of your life, **yet you cut me each day.**
8. **Alas! for the worship cast vainly** away.
9. **The key-note that** harmony whispers **to love,**
  Binding friendship **on earth, blessing spirits above.**

B.

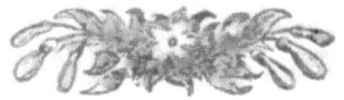

No. 51.

1st Oct., 1865.

Ulysses—Nestor—both in me combine,
Experience, wisdom, prudence, all are mine.
Yet though applauding millions greet my fame,
No temple shall perpetuate my name.

Crown me with laurels? I'm above all bays!
Contending nations vie to sound my praise.
A monarch's son, I've gained on his renown,
And for my race have won a matchless crown.

1. The scourges once of men on land and water
   We dragged our victims oft to stripes and slaughter.
2. Where the fierce and swarthy Moslem met the foe in bloody fray,
   Long the mem'ry shall be cherished of that great triumphal day.
3. In sweetest numbers once was sung my name,
   To me the poet owes a deathless fame.
4. Lo! in old ocean's coral caves I sleep
   The fairest of the dwellers of the deep.

5. We are an ancient race, **our history**
   Involved in chronicles **of mystery.**
6. There is no balm in Gilead, no relief
   To sooth **her sorrow,** to assuage her **grief.**
   Nought **here is** heard save cries **of wild** despair,
   And frantic wailings **pierce the pitying air.**
7. When western discords made **you** quake with fear,
   I from the east **send** tidings **of good cheer.**
8. **Here march my lord and lady side by** side,
   Here struts **the stately peacock in his pride.**
9. "**All is not gold that** glitters," **you may see**
   That Proverb well exemplified in me.
10. While of the **bovine** herd **I was the guest.**
    'Twas well **we** suffered not from Rinderpest.

H.

No. 52.

Invaded Turkey's best ally
When sure **dismemberment is nigh**
   My lordly first thou art.
Two meanings **in my second live,**
Compliant **and** imperative.
   My whole is but **a part.**

1. Draw up the net it will repay thy pain.
2. The mother spent her brooding care in vain.
3. New wine is apt to act upon the brain.

         O.

No. 53.

Close to the fire I love to say.
E'en on a warm oppressive day.

Descended from a lordly line,
Well fitted in Hyde Park to shine.

1. An honoured name by me was won
 With Falkland and with Algernon.
2. A strange incongruous medley I
 Of things most contradictory.
3. Well are they named the " Gate of Tears"
 Those straits the sailor trembling nears.

         O'C.

No. 54.

My first derives his title from the tomb.
My second's products heighten beauty's bloom.
My whole let no one but my first assume.

    1. I check the gout.
    2. I banish doubt.
    3. Not Smith, but **Jones**.
    4. I battered stones.

R.

No. 55.

My second—I have seen him **oft**
    And heard his plaintive note,
When from his airy perch aloft,
    He poured his little throat.
But one thing I have never seen,
    And, should I chance to see,
It were a curious sight I ween—
    That he **my** first should be.
And yet the union **must exist**,
    Because, however strange,
I've seen it figure in the list
    Of many a threatened change.

And many an oracle I've known,
  Proclaiming it as doom,
Who now in riper years has grown
  To shudder at the broom.

1. To sailors dear, to members very dear.
2. The startled waiting woman's glad surprise.
3. That rogue the Major lies in hiding here.
4. A captain given to languish and to lies.
5. A fallen fortune sure once more to rise.

O.

No. 56.

Two men who seek a common goal,
To raise, to purify the soul.
Too often waste two noble lives
While each against the other strives.
For though their labours, if combined,
Might doubly benefit mankind,
Their jealousies to evil wrest
All that is noblest, purest, best.

1. The greatest of **orators railed** at my **first**.
2. My second Italians would seize if they durst.
3. From the third we get saucepans of every size.
4. And the fourth are in London oft made into pies.
5. The fifth was a faithful and famous esquire.
6. **And the** sixth is an object of common desire.

F.

No. 57.

Where the voice of the battle is sounding afar,
   O ! there we are sure to be,
And closely united I trow we are,
For though parted in peace, we are wedded in war,
   And honoured companions we.
Say what shall the conquering brave requite,
   When the battle is hushed on the plain?
Sure vict'ry ne'er proffers a guerdon more bright
Than when damosel gives her own true knight
   The first of my noble twain.

And the second is hung where trophies teem
   In the lofty sounding hall,
Where morion, and hauberk, and target gleam
  Mid the spoils of the forest, the spoils of the stream,
   On the century-sombered wall.

1. A woman taught how bachelors should woo.
2. All-trying absence ever proves me true.
3. A sweet child's name let novel readers guess.
4. I ever stop while all things else progress.

                                            K.

No. 58.

I burst and splutter and the schoolboy please,
I sneer, abuse, and politicians tease.

Said to be made in heaven, though marred on earth,
And named from Lucifer my day of birth.

  1. I work, work, work, and never tire,
     And can't get on without my fire.

2. Through Afric **I scamper,** and hate to **be tamed,**
   I'm voted **a** donkey, though not **to be blamed.**
3. Among the **swells** I take my place,
   Though Burke himself can't tell my race.
4. **He wandered in** the fields at eventide
   And watched, and waited for his unknown bride.
5. Fiddle-de-dee ! I can very well **see**
   This is **all nonsense** you're **talking** to me.

O'E.

No. 59.

I.

Never does greatest merit
   Love its own praise to sound,
And with pretentious outcry
   The least of me is found.
By much of me collected
   Bucolic purses swell,
But pray don't let your intellects
   Join the pursuit as well.

II.

Sir J. P. Wilde, at Westminster,
   Is lord of married life,
Twixt man and wife he judges,
   And terminates their strife.
But where my use is frequent,
   Never can erring fair
Do any further mischief,
   When trusted to my care.

III.

See! on his humble pallet
   The jaded student lies,
And gloomy care dispelling,
   Sleep seals his weary eyes.
My whole in brilliant vision
   Appears to be his own,
But morning comes—he wakens—
   And finds the glory flown!

1. My truth persuades, my falsehood shocks,
   I'm often found within a box.

2. Made succulent with **garlic-clove**,
   Me, greasy **me**, the Spaniards love!
3. Life without me you well may say is **low**,
   Yet, with disease, I am your deadly foe.
4. **He** swears his truth **by** all the stars above,
   And welcomes me, the guerdon of his love!

No. 60.

What varied fortunes they **may** share
Who felt the same fond mother's care!
How one to distant marts may roam,
And one all idly lag at home!
How one may taste the rich repast
The while another's left to fast!
And **one** again accuse **his fate**
In bitter words, disconsolate!
The legend of my first may tell,
A theme that suits my second well;
That half-pathetic comic tale
Beyond all others hits the nail.
I've seen when it was told anew
My second touched and tickled too.

1. Measures, not men! be still the patriot's cry.
2. Do you but finish this and I'm your debtor.
3. The word that tells of bidding done am I.
4. And as to me, obey me—you had better.

O.

No. 61.

With a thunder crash, and a lightning flash,
   And a rent, as of cerements torn,
Torn with a fierce and convulsive gash.
   My mystical all was born.
And when the joyous feast is spread,
   That crowns the merry ball,
'Tis taken, and my first is said.
   My second, and my all.

1. A slang word I, some say 'tis shame
   For ladies slang to say or use,
  Full well I know one noble dame
   To count'nance me will ne'er refuse.

2. A well-known novelist **describes**
    Two races neath a southern **sun**;
 Of these two celebrated tribes
    I name the gentler, kindlier one.
3. I, least of all, should fear the day,
    Avoid the light, or dread disgrace,
 Yet look, and you must find alway
    Two hands are crossed **before** my face.

K.

No. 62.

"Some other form has charmed his **sight**,
   Some other face is dear,
As guerdon take this jewel bright,
   And bring my lost love here."
Thus spake the maiden to my first,
   And said, with jealous heart,
"What's now too winning make **accurst**,
   And hate for love impart."
"Yes! that will I," my first replied,
   " My second's mystic sway
Will bring thy lover **to thy side**,
   No more from **thee to stray**."

1. Mid bleak Antarctic ice go, seek my race.
2. My puny form do men grotesquely trace.
3. I mark fair Angelina's dwelling-place.
4. I shield from cold the lean Carthusian's face.
5. My festivals the Crystal Palace grace.

           T.

No. 63.

They say I'm of ignoble line,
 But spurn the base belief!
For a ballad tells how once was mine
 The blood of border chief.
Ignoble! 'twas my second called
 A city's sons to guard her,
And unto souls in slumber thralled
 Restored their ancient ardour.

   1. Half a morass.
   2. Ate what is grass.
   3. Nurse of a god.
   4. Huge in a cod.
   5. Cupid, you stupid!

           K.

No. 64.

Far, far away o'er the clear blue sea
   My first speeds fast on its way,
On, on it sweeps in the noontide heat
   And under the moon's mild ray.
But see ! what a change comes o'er it now,
   It encircles the great and strong
With so tender a care that of it bereft
   You would find them all die ere long.
Oh ! refuse it not, for 'tis fraught with good,
   Though bitter by many reckoned,
And ungrateful men will too often say
   That my first is worse than my second.

1. With Tucker (not old Daniel) met.
2. A hungry, brutal, savage, set.
3. It comes when human toils have ceased.
4. They fly me most who fly me least.

                             R.

No 65.

Full on my second in triumph burst
The holy rage of my glorious first.
And now united they stand alone
The proudest token of Britain's throne.

1. Nobles, and peasants, and kings we see
   Selling their bodies and souls for me.
2. I can change my shape, and thrust myself in,
   And turn the most godly things to a sin.
3. I dont pique myself on my words, but in fact
   You must judge by my notes, and my every act.
4. Ah ! golden link, of which poets sing,
   May not the bird of love take wing ?
5. Leave me, leave me, you may not stay,
   The whistle is shrieking—away ! away !
6. The greatest loss since time began
   That ever befell the race of man.

No. 66.

Within my heart my black **first** lies.
My second rivets earthly ties.
My whole, the cause of all man's sighs,
Was beauty's far **most** famous prize.

1. Me Thomas took, and 'twas his latest view.
2. First word to cheer **the** London-lost " Mossoo."
3. The greatest friend that mankind ever knew.

K.

No. 67.

He said " on such a night as this "—
   That moonlight scene—you know **it**—
The fairest page of human bliss
   Pourtrayed by pen of poet.
When home to Belmont's friendly **towers**
   The young **Lorenzo** brought her,
And whiled away the happy **hours**
   With **Shylock's pretty** daughter;
Until their playfulness became
   Absorbed in deeper feeling,
When towards my first at length there came
   My second gently stealing.

The tale would please me more, I own,
    If, while eloping thither,
Lorenzo stole his bride alone,
    And not the ducats with her.
Ah! had he but possessed my whole,
    And that in ample measure,
He might not then have stained his soul
    With Shylock's ill-got treasure.
As to my whole—I cannot say
    If Shylock ever saw it—
But from his brethren of to-day,
    It is the deuce to draw it.

1. In Scotland, like Achilles' dart,
    I give, and then assuage, a smart.
2. Though not a miser, 'tis my fate
    For ever to accumulate.
3. Let Piron's epitaph apply,
    Qui ne fut rien, for so say I.
4. I'm very little of a bore,
    Yet none divides the commons more.

                                O.

No. 68.

The fish are dead that lie my depths within.
To night's pale child I owe my origin.
My first doth " vex the drowsy ear of night."
My second is the first of banquet bright.

      1. A bill and coo.
      2. Good-bye to you,
      3. Attained by few.

K.

No. 69.

My second in my first doth dwell,
Nay more, my whole ('tis strange to tell)
Lives, like my second, in my first,
Therein as in a cradle nursed.
My first's a female always reckoned,
And little cares she for my second ;
Whereas all females, save this one,
My second to desire are prone.
Again, my second doth with glee
My first in gallant company,
And then rejoices in his soul
Within my first to meet my whole.

1. When the Christians in the fortress broke the Moslem legions down,
   Then an ancient race recovered what they once had won—a crown.
2. Seek me, seek me, where the Bulbul makes the night more dear than day,
   With the magic of his music in the blushes of Cathay.
3. The golden calf stood gleaming in the noon-tide torrid glow,
   Anon in dust it grovelled from the fury of my blow.
4. I vowed to love and faithful be to my long absent lord,
   And spite of traitors and of wiles, I kept my plighted word.

H.

No. 70.

A patriot in youth's brightest hour
Of country's love showed forth the power:
With high-born courage nobly clad,
My first for him no terrors had.

Regardless of home's warning **voice,**
My second **made** for love **his choice** :
" **He** could **not** see, he could not hear,
Or sound or sign forboding fear."
His love was chivalrous and pure,
His death was sudden—premature.
" **That tale** is old, but love anew
May teach young hearts to prove as true."
As to my whole—the selfish crowd
With efforts strong, and clamour lou**d,**
Use every means to gain their ends
Even to the detriment of friends,
For everyone directs his labours
To rise o'er shoulders of his neighbours.

   1. **A** second word unite to me
      And, lo ! a brilliant poem see.
   2. **Ever** in life the battle-cry
      Of him who wins the victory.
   3. **A schoolman, and** of reverend fame,
      As son **of mine I justly claim,**
   4. In fact, I'm nice **to eat and** tender,
      Ironically tough as fender.

R.

No. 71.

My first it flashes in the brook,
   It gilds the glittering spire,
It tesselates with varied tints
   The gloomy minster choir.
And when my first with rosy lips
   Doth kiss the morning dew,
The virgin drops return its love,
   And blush my second's hue.

1. Dear prefix sought through toiling days.
2. The king of beasts obeyed my voice.
3. I'm often ruled in legal phrase.
4. Oft used the symbol of a choice.
5. The falling tide is named from mine,
6. Sweet lay! all things in thee rejoice.
7. Procrastination's chosen time.

                                     T.

No. 72.

In music's softest strains my first should reign,
 And yet too oft it doth foul discord raise.
My second seek where, amid grandest strain,
 "The pealing anthem swells the note of praise."

1. " Praise undeserved is satire in disguise."
2. Lip service in song-loving Italy.
3. What in a lover every maid should prize.
4. What every careful wife to be should try.
5. What ofttimes soothes the wildest agony.

R.

No. 73.

The first betimes was mighty, mild;
The last nor old nor yet a child.
The whole by revolution strained
The bonds by which it was enchained.

1. In me you seek a peerless prize.
2. What some must swallow.
3. What all must follow.
4. Triumphant o'er the wave we rise.

F.

No. 74.

I.
The lazy swell was sent to me,
My works and hilly home to see.

II.
Four threaded fences, neatly drawn,
Enclose and mete the perfect lawn.

III.
What surging waves of unseen fire
Fill apse and transept, nave and choir!

    1. Spans triumph's throng.
    2. Inspire each song.
    3. An Oxford gong.

No. 75.

Now o'er my first with headlong speed,
    Through smoky towns, by meadows bright,
Swifter than fleetest Arab steed,
    My second's borne in onward flight.
Beneath my first—above no more—
    My second lies—no trumpet's sound,
No loudest cannon's angry roar
    Shall e'er disturb its rest profound.

1. See in the lake beneath a summer sky
   The ivied ruin clearly imaged lie!
2. A bonded spirit first, then duty free.
3. We help to make things plain all must agree.
4. The river murmurs peacefully along,
   Where once a poet led the rustic song.
5. May every gentle wife and maid escape
   Alike my disposition and my shape!
6. Ah! craftsman bold, those dizzy summits fly,
   Lest thy blood too the treacherous snows
      should dye.
7. Whose birth and death alike, ah! cruel fate!
   A heedless world is taught to celebrate.

R.

No. 76.

I.

Though justice halt—though Nemesis may fail—
To me belongs the even balanced scale.

II.

I'm counted haughty, I am cold, I know,
And scarce can fail, amid a waste of snow.

III.

To ask for me may equally portend
The entrance to a quarrel or its end.

1. 'Tis I should lead the present hairy fashion.
2. I killed my son in just, though jealous passion.
3. Dear to the Turk and me is the Circassian.

O.

No. 77.

To a five and a ten add a musical A,
And the name of my first shall reward your essay.
If further my fair one you vain would pursue,
In the twelfth of my second she gladdens your view.

1. I'm drawn by horses, and by heroes led.
2. A six and five I symbolize, 'tis said.
3. A giant I, I finish two like me.
4. In me a proud but jilted maiden see.
5. As provident as little busy bee.

K.

No. 78.

Emblem of purity my first—sign of disease and pain.
My second recks not of his life if he my first may gain.

1. Pray spare the stick, poor Ned will trot along
   At this one word, at least so says the song.
2. "Even in our ashes live their wonted fires,"
   And warlike sons avenge their slaughtered sires.
3. I am no monarch, but you'll all agree
   A noble Don is swallowed up by me.
4. The early trumpet sounds its shrill alarm,
   And calls upon each warrior bold to arm.
5. I'm little noted, save that it was mine
   To help to keep a witty, mad, Divine.

R.

No. 79.

When hoary mullion mars the pallid moon,
    And breaks her glance o'er chancel, nave, and cell,
I steal me forth in midnight's ghastly noon,
    And tread the haunts where buried heroes dwell.
My reign is short; appeared, I vanish soon,
    My fairest form, the Dame of Avenel!

I'm red and hot, and ever lurk with him
    Who showed Don Cleophas those varied views;
With stout De Bouillon linked, jet armour trim
    And round as Norval's shield I wholly use.
I'm white as foam reed-caught on river brim,
    And fall as fine as Summer evening dews.

       1. Caught up by three to one.
       2. Sweet when swain's day is done.
       3. Single a sound of dun,
       4. Fond of malicious fun.
       5. Circumlocution spun.
       6. What ne'er should do true gun.

                                          K.

No. 80.

My first beneath an evil star was **born**,
Sport of the winds and waters, eve and morn.
Look on my first and you my second see,
A noted scene of fearful anarchy.

1. **Store** up the wine.
2. **I'd like to dine!**
3. Beats measured chime.
4. The olden time.

R.

No. 81.

I.

Friend **of** " **the** Dodger," Charley Bates,
Jack Sheppard, and congenial mates.

II.

Although **I** conquer many hearts,
When **I appear** all love **departs.**

III.

While pacing through my lordly halls,
A humbler dwelling thought **recalls.**

1. I north and south together tie.
2. The lambkin plays **me skittishly.**
3. **Now** white, now **black,** now point am I.

K.

No. 82.

Although I never acted, danced, nor sung,
    Yet on the stage to go I ne'er did fail,
No knight am I, yet royal arms were hung
    About me, and I carried royal mail.

I am no limner, yet I often drew,
    And though no coward, oft I ran away.
I never laugh, yet some say that I do.
    I never game, yet men dislike my play.
I never save, yet many call me near,
    And some will say I'm off, when on the road;
And though from party politics quite clear,
    On me the name of leader is bestowed.

    1. Where Quakers never go.
    2. Through sunny lands I flow.
    3. Revived in Lord Mayor's show.
    4. Most difficult to sew.
    5. I make good soup I know.

    H.

No. 83.

My first may reign, as poets say,
Queen of the brilliant and the gay.
And many a knight on bended knee
May swear eternal fealty.
My second is her subject true,
Returns each glance with brightness new.
And while it serves with prompt subjection,
Gives many a moment to reflection.
Alas! that time with " wasting finger,"
Forbids such happiness to linger,
Destroys my first with fatal blow,
And turns my next from friend to foe.
Poor victims injured and betrayed
Call Madame Rachel to your aid;
Her arts may bid you yet agree,
And triumph in your unity.

1. Child of the sun I bring you light,
   Yet prop your houses by my might.
2. A Parliament that long subsisted,
   Ere Rome or Westminster existed.
3. Seek Ireland through, and seek again,
   You look for such as me in vain.

4. "To those about to marry," come,
   And let me decorate your home.
5. 'Tis sweet when voices twain unite—
   When three combine, ah! what delight!
6. An old friend tried and understood,
   May my successor prove as good!   B.

No. 84.

When left to myself I'm as dark as the night,
With the aid of my second how dazzling my light!

As a prisoner I'm useful, so don't set me free,
For if I escape, in bad odour you'll be.

1. Though I hope I may ne'er be without thee, I own,
   May I ne'er be within thee, thou demon of stone!
2. When a savant proclaims to the public his science,
   He shouldn't set decency's laws at defiance.
3. Uncertain are most things, we're taught, here below,
   But we are too certain, as most of you know.

R.

No. 85.

I.

As the fire burns clear and bright,
    And the moments quickly pass,
With mellow wine let each delight
    In merry vein to fill his glass.

II.

Ever foremost in the fight
    Where each resolves to do or die,
'Tis surely then a glorious sight
    The crest of valour to descry.

III.

"In the watches of the night,"
    "When the stormy winds do blow,"
A sudden cry! a sound of fright!
    Too late to shun impending woe.

1. Now wielding the sceptre, now nursing the snake.
2. I keep my composure and holiday take.
3. And "rest and be thankful" is my motto too.
4. The king took his breakfast, and then said adieu.

F.

No. 86.

About the twain you hear and read
    Such curious contradictions,
That, though familiar things indeed,
    You might suppose them fictions.
My first—you find it takes no less
    Than forty men to make it,
And yet it seems like wretchedness
    To want it or forsake it.
Nor can you greater praise bestow
    Than firm and staunch to term it,
And yet 'tis said to overflow—
    The papers all affirm it.
Beside, around, or near my first
    My second is delightful,
And yet 'tis "fatal" and "accursed,"
    With other terms as frightful.
" 'Tis all we long for," gently sigh
    The humble and retiring—
" 'Tis all we pant for," loudly cry
    The forward and aspiring.

Of science once in high request,
  Each was a handmaid reckoned,
Astrology my first possessed,
  And heraldry my second.

1. I am the Sultan's mandate to his slaves.
2. The Sultan's dreaded rival rules my waves.
3. A fascinating creature on the whole,
   But, like some other fair ones, wanting soul.
4. "Sire, for my love break through the foreign chain;"
5. I **lost a realm** thereby—how **great my gain**!

O.

No. 87.

I.
By many chastenings vainly tried.

II.
A symbol of eternity.

III.
The twain **allied**,
The fire test plied,
A mountain from a molehill **I**.

1. Ire arches my back.
2. How doubles my track !
3. A futurity peeper.
4. A very long sleeper.
5. The first of the pack.
6. Makes Momus a weeper.
7. Tops Chang, or Anak.

K.

No. 88.

When we two meet together, turn and see,
For nothing lovelier on earth can be.
Beauty is ours, bright with a heavenly glow,
But transient as all beauty here below.

1. Quoth savage, " Mother's deity, alas !
   A mightier wizard doth in power surpass."
2. There's magic in this word to do or dare,
   To heighten pleasure, or to lighten care.
3. Be not discouraged if you find me hard,
   My inner worth is not by hardness marred.

R.

No. 89.

My first was formed to bear the weight
   Of an Imperial crown,
And they who **prize** its high estate
   Might prize it more when down.

For what has all **the** past bequeathed
   That touches man **more** near?
To it the fairest queen that breathed
   Was fain to bend an **ear.**

Its thought **though** dissipation's throng
   In giddy hours adjourn,
Upon it vainly pondering long
   The sagest head will **turn.**

For it the temples **from of** old
   Were decked in fit array,
Though now **they lie** all bare and cold;
   So progress points the way.

My second is their darling theme
   Who toil for praise **or** pence:
It is the broken soldier's dream,
   The minister's **pretence.**

A wish that all or feel or feign,
  By some too early nursed;
Yet woe to them who seek in vain
  To find it in my first.

1. A pseudo-savage, and a lettered cheat.
2. How, when a boy, I scorned this trading traitor!
3. A noble head, but lines diverging meet.
4. For stony guest a most unwilling waiter.
5. The desert's kindly ships my verdure greet.
6. A very awkward and unskilful skater.

O.

No. 90.

A brief conjunction binds us to proclaim
The farmer's glory, and the parson's shame.
The farmer's glory when his crops are we,
The parson's shame when we're his homily.

1. Theme of many a rumination.
2. Left me for a new plantation.
3. Angular in explanation.

I. H.

No. 91.

A forward maiden, pretty, pert,
   And buoyant, bright as early hope,
Too old to play, too young to flirt,
And yet in either art expert,
   Now partner plies—now skipping rope.

How many a pleasant one we've had,
   Old friend, your dear hand clasped in mine!
And yet if but the first we add,
A trivial jargon, senseless, *fade*,
   The magpie talking 'neath the pine!

1. Fit cuttings these for wisdom teeth.
2. "The favorite wins!" resounds the Heath.
3. The pride of indolent Maggiore.
4. Involved the thread of Dickens' story.

                                    K.

No. 92.

The lady coyly joined the mazy dance,
Her husband twirled his thumbs and looked askance;
But, soon excited by the tabor's sound,
He rose, and gaily wheeled in merry round.

This sun in leafy June shines o'er the lea;
This fire at Christmas all with rapture see;
These fond smiles gladden, and *these* black eyes glisten;
And spell-bound thousands to *this* tribune listen.

1. Initials of a high, but modern court.
2. I of both kings and bishops made rare sport.
3. The player first in this performs his part,
4. Then stings the guilty sinner to the heart.
5. My monarch was a wondrous man to wive.
6. My scourge scarce left a single beast alive.

H.

No. 93.

My first precedes a fall, yet who denies
A pardon to it is nor good nor wise.
It often makes my second, when in fume
The cleanly housewife sees her sullied room.
Combined my first and second form that style
Which Blanches love, and Warringtons revile.

1. In ladies' hands the tenderest ties I **sever**.
2. A lady once, the **victor's** prize for ever.
3. A lady once, and high, then **low**.
4. A sly half glance which **I can ne'er** forego.

I. H.

No. 94.

Divided, we still must be one,
And an article just in your sight,
Our **union**, division begun
Between man **and his earliest** delight.

1. Father of many a harmless jest.
2. Seek me when Phœbus sinks to rest.

I. H.

No 95.

I.
But a letter is lost since the olden time
   When I sheltered the nun as she told her beads,
The ancient age of the Catholic prime,
   Ere the strife began of contending creeds.

II.
Come hither my love, and wander with me
   Where the breath of the roses is sweetly blown,
Where the fruits and the flowers are fair to see,
   When the shadow of black bat night hath flown.

III.
The flowers are plucked, they are gone to pot,
   And dished are the fruits the flowers among,
But the black bat night to the place hath brought
   The fruits of music, the flowers of song.

1. Castled I check the kingly stream.
2. The wolf's long howl, the poet's dream.
3. Those evening bells, Sicilian, gory.
4. The best edition, folio, Doré.
5. From tears I turn a heartless rock.
6. The cannon's mouth I fearless block.

                              F.

No. 96.

Rats, mice, and men alike my first consume:
Kings make my last, yet beggars there find room.
One will alone a master's power obey,
And yet the other owns a woman's sway.
Both can redress a wrong no laws can cure,
Yet one gives laws that seldom long endure.
In one the wisdom of an age is read,
Yet one by foolish counsels oft is led.
One doth a king's dishonor oft display,
Yet both show forth his honor every day.

1. A murderous fanatic was I.
2. A murderer too, of deepest dye.
3. A something larger than a fly.
4. A sage that read the human eye.
5. A race extinct, a rule gone by.

M.

No. 97.

Though my first be a signal of woe,
   It is short, I am sure, to the letter.
Though my second be bad, you may go
   To a hazard in getting a better.
My whole from the East in a bark
   You may see growing white from the tossing,
Though in London at noon he is dark,
   And seems quite at home at the crossing.

1. I'm opposed to the cleric alone.
2. I'm a charm pretty commonly known.
3. You make me when you're out of your own.

I. H.

No. 98.

Republican, gory.
In Chili my glory.
Reformer, or Tory.

1. A motley fate.
2. I've sisters eight.
3. A thirsty state.

R.

No. 99.

My first's a man, so called by **every tongue**
In Rome itself, when **Rome** itself was young
A man like him the Mantuan poet sung.

My second too **was** potent in its day,
Strong to subdue, but seldom let to stray,
Unless **when stricter duty oped** the way.

Without my first is virtue incomplete—
Without my last less vice were in the street—
In both combined is something pure and sweet.

My second **fills the** palace with alarms,
Flies from the Crown, or from a Prince's **arms**,
U**pon** a beggar to bestow her charms.

My **first is** often mentioned by the teacher—
My **second** oft discouraged **by the** preacher—
My **first and** last combined **a** matchless creature.

Without my first no marriage vows are said,
My **second** needs the **license to be read**,
My whole, **that** is the **two, is never wed**.

   1. The Scalded dog let this disclose.
   2. A town Gaeta's hills inclose.
   3. Punch, **question,** letters, candles, nose.   M.

No. 100.

My first was the cause, I remember well,
  That my spirit beneath my second fell,
While my whole, of a Scottish name the pride,
  Has over and over my first defied.

1. I'm close and cross, and, I confess,
   An antient go-between.
2. A foe to progress, yet no less
   Do I, when fairly weighed, express
   A coming change of scene.
3. At times the soldier's, and I fear
   At other times the devil's.
4. A frowning fortress, tier on tier
   O'erlooks a city's revels.
5. Come, crown the work you proudly rear,
   But look to lines and levels.

O.

No. 101.

Whither I would have you fly
We when parted signify.
What when parted you must write,
We to signify unite.

1. What your robe must be for you,
   But what you must never do.
2. Genuine offspring of the Earth,
   Pure when emblem of your worth.

I. H.

No. 102.

Fair stranger from a brighter sphere,
Condemned to smile and suffer here!
One cruel touch—and we may know
Thy kinsmen, and thy deadliest foe.

1. Restrained and leagued by this in one firm band.
2. Insane she died, with flowers in either hand.
3. Modest and sweet, what scent rewards the winner!
4. The centre of the gravity of dinner.

B.

No. 103.

Unlike the storied keep of Ross
    That sentinels the broad Lough Lene,
Made hoar with lichens, ferns and moss,
    With emblematic ivy, green,
My hue is of the dome above,
    And though a ruin I am strong,
My spirit, fierce as Paynim's love,
    Illumes the palace, blights the throng.

1. Some stick at naught—but I at every one.
2. In me a sort of substitution view.
3. Where reigns white Aphrodite charmed to stone.
4. With "oaten stop" hear gentle Collins woo.

                                        K.

No. 104.

I.

Gentle and loving, harsh and rude,
Heavy or light, as suits the mood !
The pealing organ's notes I wake,
And by the painter's art I make
The canvas live with graces rare
Of glowing form, or landscape fair.
Though oft met in disdainful beauty,
Yet often 'tis my menial duty,
Steeled to the task, in pride's despite
The beggar's blackened pipe to light.
With tender hand the mother mild
Can give me to her sleeping child :
And yet I fly, with terror crowned,
The messenger of death around.

II.

A varied lot is also mine,
And many forms in me combine.
At times I'm free, yet ever dwell
A prisoner in the felon's cell.

Now in the vast cathedral dome,—
Now in the humblest peasant's home—
Now in the alpine realms of snow—
Now in the ocean's depths below.
Buried in earth, yet sent from heaven,
Thrown to the dogs—to beauty given.
Toiled for in vain in by-gone age,
A priceless gain to anxious sage!
Now found by infant hands, unsought,
And cast away without a thought.

III.

Fantastical through woodland glades
I ministered to errant maids;
And kept my watch beneath the tree,
And fortune found no friend in me.
"By Celia's Arbour" all the day,
Though not in glee, 'twas mine to stay.
My garments tawdry were to see,
My love was tawdry to a T.
Thus far in play—but, leaving jest,
I am a friend your friends to test;
My trying virtue, in good sooth,
Points to the false, unveils the truth.

1. Contact with pitch defiles, 'tis said,
   But pitch with me will turn the head.
2. Act such as this will give good reason
   Why juries should convict of treason.
3. A city, in Italian borders,
   Reared a divine, though not in orders.
4. I dwell the kingly courts within,
   And yet I'm not too proud to spin.
5. Cold and pure, of heavenly birth,
   Short-lived dweller upon earth.

R.

No. 105.

I.

In Ireland by a lever raised,
　　With Charles he served in Spain,
That lever's power he oft amazed,
　　In Erin back again.
He's ever jolly, never triste,
　　And welcome guest *quand même*,
He only sits at any feast
　　A mere *quatorzième*.

II.

The gallant knight **my** plural suits,
  Though mimic **war** they be:
The pantaloon it little **boots**
  My singular to see.
Attention oft 'tis mine to force,
  As those who've done me know—
When civil, from my ample source
  Both wealth and honor flow.

III.

The Habeas Corpus take away,
  We have a right the less—
Suspending me makes England pay,
  But spares her chartered press.
But when the stars have passed away,
  Their golden reign all over,
Then frugal folks go forth to play,
  And think themselves in clover.

1. Inclined to chaff, I give no real pain,
   Although, I own, I go against the grain.
2. Barbers are famed as gossips, each one knows,
   And this great name the Barber will disclose.
3. The comic poet gave the frogs,
   While went the tragic to the dogs.
4. A French word anglicized—I mean
   A sweet and dainty go between.

R.

No. 106.

I.

Not up or down,—to left or right,
  Through life's eventful day;
'Tis thus we find the Christian's light,
  In this the Christian's way.

II.

Primeval darkness veiled the sky,
  And robed the deep below—
A wanderer since then am I,
  A pilgrim to and fro.

III.

The rugged paths of toil are blessed
With glimpses of the hour of rest.

1. I'm felt when **pretty cousins cozen**.
2. Two letters equal **half a** dozen.
3. There dawned the light that shineth **o'er us**.
4. We see it not though straight **before us**.

'C.

No. 107.

A word—and my first awakes,
   In the face of the young and bright;
A blow—and its lustre breaks
   In the hearthstone's flickering light.
Far hidden from human eye
   My second the grasses shroud,
Yet it lures its thousands to die
   And conquers the great and proud.

1. My first again, too charming to forsake.
2. Pale spirits wander o'er a lifeless lake.
3. What man alone is patented to make.
4. My second for my last I needs must take.

                              E.

No. 108.

The pure and icy mid-night air
Exalted, while it chilled, our veins;
As on we trod in silence there,
Five thousand feet above the plains:
And yet, five thousand feet above,
In robe of everlasting white,
Its diadem the star of Jove,
My first soared glorious to the right.
My second from the deep abyss
Which yawned as though the earth were cleft
Down to the very throne of Dis,
Rose dark and spectral on the left.

The wicked charm its course shall run,
Although forbid to end in death,
For eighty weary weeks and one,
With paling blood, and poisoned breath.
In food untouched, in slumber fled,
In storms pursuing o'er the brine,
The sentence of the hag is read
Expressed in these two words of mine.

1. Impelling and restraining forces
   Launched it on its whirling courses.
2. Christian knight and Moslem sleeping,
   Madman saint his vigils keeping.
3. Awful principle of ill!
   Myriads hold thy doctrine still.
4. Trust not color, graceful boy,
   But my varied tints employ.

O.

No 109.

If my whole were my second, the girls of my first
Would be dressed in the fashion, as now, if they durst.

1. The child of the air and the child of the sea,
   And well they know why, are in terror of me.
2. For the stage, or the church; neither drama nor ode,
   But a mixture to make of religion the mode.
3. I'm made up of hundreds, and yet am but one,
   To go to my quarters I double a stone.

I. H.

No. 110.

I mused beneath the Christmas holly
   And dreamed of by-gone yules,
Till my heart became as far from jolly
   As azure is from gules.
And I heard a far-off sound awaking
   Thoughts tender—hard to bear;
And the holy Christmas morn was breaking
   With music in the air.
My mood that morn—that sad sweet pealing—
   To name a flower unite,
Whose gay tints through the shadow stealing
   To darkest dells give light.

1. I really am the very deuce!
2. Sans me the public is no use.
3. Mere mountains—see the Gazetteers.
4. Pray grant me strawberry-leaves and spheres.

                         K.

No. 111.

Young Cupid once in frolic cried,
  "Now Hymen do your best"—
He plucked my first in mimic pride,
  And stuck it in his crest.
But Hymen from Olympian bowers
  Came where the boy stood mute:
He crowned him with my second's flowers,
  And fed him with the fruit.

1. Unrivalled he pursued the even tenor of his way.
2. A little further, further yet, why do ye seek to stay?
3. The pride of many a stately head now in the dust laid by.
4. I hide below, "the Cornish boys may know the reason why."
5. Old Æsop tells how they of old thankless abused my reign,
6. But this they never found again beneath their new King Crane.

B.

No. 112.

When light went forth, and God's command
  The gates of darkness burst,
And life was dawning o'er the land,
  Creation was my first;
And people say the happy soul
Who has my second has my whole.

  1. Though very fatal to the foe
    I can't abide the sturgeon's roe.
  2. On every side it meets the sight,
    In gay saloons and halls of light.
  3. It helps to make the crooked straight,
    The lame forget his limping gait.
  4. I come before the morning ray,
    And follow the decline of day.

                           M'C.

No. 113.

I

Though like a noble marquis—very,
    I take the name of Vane,
And Tempest follows—Londonderry,
    I am not your Thane.

II.

I laugh through ferny Scottish wood,
    And leap from crag to cairn;
The home of silvery darting brood,
    And playmate of each bairn.

III.

Too weak the first of these light things
    Their union to survive,
Yet joined—in chiefest place of kings,
    To reign the two contrive.

1. Should Acrosticians stoop to me,
   In me entrapped I trust they'll be.
2. "Where can I find this puzzling pair?"
   I asked in French, Monsieur said, "where!"

3. A circle ends not, 'tis propounded;
   Then, O! why he who circled round it?
4. **A hall of** joyaunce, go, **my** slaves,
   And rear beside these caverned waves!

K.

No. 114.

I.

The filming eye in death **so meek,**
The big tear stilled upon the cheek,
The woodbine **by** the antlers torn,
And interwoven with them worn,
Each tells of death, would bid us mourn,
Save for the wild exulting **cheer,**
The joyous pack of chiming hounds,
And ringing through our forest here
These duly taught **sweet** woodland sounds.

II.

With chance allied 'tis always sought,
   And hazard gives it rein,
'Tis ever crossed (though curbless thought)
   For glory **or** for gain.

In two ways it is often set,
   To fatal fight now driven,
Now like the child the poet met,
   "O master, it is seven."

III.

Its numbing hand with icy clasp
Would fain the smiling pastures grasp;
What acts of man, how manifold,
To keep these pastures from its hold!

1. When I'm the word no sound is heard.
2. Hear sound and sense in this.
3. O lovely lake my mirror make.
4. The Nabob's noonday bliss.

K.

No. 115.

I.

When **autumn** nights grow chill,
   And storms the upland sweep,
On a bleak and lonely **hill**
   I **lay me** down to sleep:
But I laugh at the surging wind,
   As it rocks me to and fro,
Safe in **my** couch reclined,
   Though **its** coverlet be **snow**.

That stormy **time is** past,
   With its blinding mist and rain:
Hushed is that wintry blast,
   I wake me **up again**!
My veil **I fling aside,**
   I smooth **my** tangled **hair,**
My breast **I** open wide
   To **woo** the genial air;
I bask in the friendly beams,
   I lap the **balmy dew,**
And a joyous **young life** streams
   My quickened pulses through.

II.

Far on the stormy Indian main
   His anxious trade the merchant plies:
O'er trampled heaps of bleeding slain,
   With ruthless stride the invader flies:
The reckless votaries of spoil
   Their myriad schemes of plunder weave;
Behold them all, with varied toil,
   Straining my second to achieve!

III.

The strangest is yet untold—
   Strangest and yet most true—
Though shut up to keep in the old,
   I open to give out the new!
By statesmen to day entertained,
   I am shouldered by tramps on the morrow;
And the nation by me is maintained,
   Though it deems me its weightiest sorrow!

1. O save me from his cruel bite!
2. A kinsman visited by night.
3. The doom of many a luckless wight!

C. W.

No. 116.

I.

Forlorn, unfriended, bowed with years,
    A wanderer wends from door to door,
And craves with scarcely hidden tears
    The slender bounty of the poor.
My faithful first his steps attends,
    Of rugged form and homely face,
Forlorn like him, bereft of friends,
    Like him, an outcast of his race.

II.

Seek for my next on the autumn field
    Where sickle and gleaner their work have done,
In the meagre heap which its gatherings yield
    To the toiler's search from sun to sun.
Or, where December's storm has passed
    With icy breath o'er the forest's side,
See the scant leaves crouching from its blast,
    Or caught aloft in its whirling tide.
Or count how often celestial spirits
    Descend to brighten this world of sin,
Foreshowing the hope which man inherits,
    Waking for heaven the voice within.

III.

The scene shifts back to an olden time,
    And a nation stricken with nameless woe,
Where the surging wave of war and crime
    Has left the track of its angry flow.
Hark! a sound ascends in the calm of even,
    Stealing soft through the languid air!
Say, does it herald the message of heaven,
    The blessed summons to peace and prayer?
Ah no! at that dread ill-omened call
    Franklin and hind in the hamlet cower;
The grim thane chafes in his darkened hall,
    The lute is hushed in the lady's bower.
No more the yeoman trims his bow,
    Stilled is the busy shuttle's sound,
The gleeman's voice is silent now,
    The cold and cheerless hearth around.
The clerk forsakes his learned lore,
    The poet leaves his lay aside;
Nor book nor lay availeth more
    Till the light of morning tide.

    1. Base recreant from the fight.
    2. An arbiter of right.
    3. Disturber of the night.   C. W.

No. 117.

I.

Said the King to his court assembled,
  "Come, name me the strongest thing,"
And they answered in turn and trembled,
  "The strongest art thou, O king."
"Nay! beauty hath kings to woo her,
  And holds them in subject thrall,"
"And wine is a world subduer,"
  "But truth shall prevail o'er all."
Yet they named not *me*, a mightier far
  Than truth, or women, or Princes are.

II.

Of a restless race descended,
  Producing a restless brood,
Who roam till their course is ended,
  Yet sluggish am I of mood.
With me combined, things good or ill
  Are brighter, and purer, or darker still.

III.

She whispered her secret, sighing,
  In a low and pleading tone,
And, her softened sire complying,
  She called me at length her own:
Yet, when I approached her, that fickle she
  So haughtily turned her back on me.

1. When you catch me you catch a Tartar.
2. Acquaintance of the royal martyr.
3. Of service in affairs of barter.
4. Esteemed companions of the garter.

                                             O.

No. 118.

I.
In towns restricted, but in counties free.

II.
We shun the gigot when we sound the T.

III.
Red, radical, green plumed, and drilled is he.

    1. The neck circumvented.
    2. Zerlina consented.
    3. Disaffect—discontented.   K.

No. 119.

My first beneath my second lies,
    My second neath my first;
One our best passion sanctifies,
    And one proclaims our worst.
Without my first we cannot live,
    By loves fond witching led,
And yet, alas! too oft we give
    My second when we're wed.
Both are chameleon to the view
    And hues alternate shed,
One takes delight in black and blue,
    And one in white and red.
One is a failure, ah! too oft,
    When help we need from it,
One never fails, for, hard or soft,
    Tis a decided hit.

1. What Saul of Tarsus made at first.
2. A place where freedom long is nursed.
3. By Muldau's stream near Dresden town.
4. The Post my failing doth renown.

No. 120.

Renowned of old for power to charm,
    In many a classic hall of pleasure;
As famous now for power to harm,
    And dealing death in murderous measure.
Say, who between us shall decide,
    Which is the deadlier, which the dearer,
The more remorseless homicide,
    The sunken heart's more potent cheerer?

      1. Smooth, but superficial.
      2. Squatting in the prairie.
      3. Garment sacrificial.
      4. Useful in the dairy.
      5. Drink of which be wary.

                                  O.

No. 121.

I.

I bend o'er my desk with troubled mien,
   With straining eyes and aching brow,
As I think of the hopes so fair yestreen,
   But alas! all dark and lowering now.
O'er balance and debit I sadly pore;
   Day-book and ledger—I scan them all:
I list, at each click of the opening door,
   How fitful markets rise and fall.
Yet, when misfortunes darkest lower,
   And care comes weariest to me,
Give me only my first one breezy hour,
   And my heart grows light and my spirit free.

II.

My second, while yet the world was new,
   Was art's first gift to man;
And men to-day the craft pursue
   With new device and plan.
See, neath the engine's ponderous shaft,
   The lengthening roll expand,
And grow, as with instinctive craft,
   At the touch of a viewless hand!

III.

I staunch the warrior's bleeding vein,
    With sure though slender band,
The struggling captive flies in vain
    From the clasp of my ruthless hand.
In the lifting mist of morning tide,
    I ride on the sleepy air,
And the laughing sunbeams glint aside
    From the sheen of my streaming hair.
Yet I lurk in the nook of the lonely wall
    Mid solitude and gloom,
Unmoved and grim, while my victims fall
    In the gaping jaws of doom.

    1. I herald the early dawn.
    2. I come when the cloth is drawn.
    3. I lurk neath the flowery lawn.

C. W.

No. 122.

I.

The solemn pageant winds along
    In slow and stately file,
Low rolls the wave of sacred song
    Adown the echoing aisle.
And as more faint the distant notes
    In dying cadence fall,
My voice, o'er all ascending, floats
    In measured interval.
And still we haunt that ancient hall,
    My brothers seven and I.
Born .neath the shadow of its wall,
    There too we, swanlike, die.
Antique and quaint the names we bear,
    Uncouth in modern eyes;
Though mine you oftentimes may hear
    In moments of surprise.

II.

When first on baby's lips it hung,
    The second thrilled my heart with pride,
Though spoken by another tongue,
    'Tis sheepishness personified.

But wherefore puzzle o'er a name
  That known is scarcely worth the trouble ?—
'Twill serve all purposes the same,
  If you will only halve its double.

III.

A king am I, supreme, alone—
  Sceptre and sword are mine;
A king, and yet a priest—my throne
  In name all but divine.
And still nor priest of holiest rite,
  Nor prince of proudest grade,
Will hold his solemn state aright,
  Save in my folds arrayed.

1. The proudest noble to my humble toil
  Is ever debtor for the coat he wears.
2. My evil deeds may yet embroil,
  And set two nations by the ears.

C. W.

DUBLIN ACROSTICS.

No. 123.

I.

Where, **neath** yon willow's waving shade,
The pleasant waters softly sigh,
My frolic first unconscious played,
Nor dreamed of doom or danger nigh.
And yet—perplexing mystery—
My first may still deserve **its name**,
E'en though a blackened mass it lie
Beneath **my** second's **breath of** flame.

II.

Enchained **full** many a fathom deep
My captive second long did dwell,
Where murky elves their vigils **keep**,
With smouldering brand, and fiery spell.
But **lo! the spell** is broken—See!
Science hath issued her **behest**,
The captive speeds o'**er land and** sea,
To every home a welcome guest.

III.

So time's **recurring cycles roll,**
 And fashion **runs its chequered race;**
My second now supplants my whole,
 And fills, or **more than fills, its** place.

And thus, capriciously defying
  The laws of geometric art,
Axioms and rules alike belying,
  The whole is lesser than its part.

1. Champion of Saxon right.
2. Foremost in every fight.
3. A blood-empurpled stream.
4. A baffled nation's dream.

C. W.

No. 124.

Praise or blame! and my whole denies
  Whatever my first affirms.
My second and first are fast allies
  And stand for the same in terms.

1. The squires and their aim.
2. When you find, you'll exclaim.

I. H.

No. 125.

I.
Though hot and fiery on the hill,
I run my course till I wax chill,
And then I stand unmoved and still.

II.
Though full of angry passions now,
When educated I can bow
To fortune, and my change avow.

III.
I cannot, Rachel-like, defy
The ravages of time, yet I
Have as my aim to beautify.

1. An oft imprisoned thing,
   And yet I sing.
2. A daily task is mine,
   And yet I shine.
3. Two simple letters see,
   Yet great are we.
4. Expensive to the land
   And yet I stand.

L.

No. 126.

I.

Two the eyes, and two the ears,
Twice one sees, and twice one hears :
One the tongue, and once alone
In the tongue is sound and tone.
Double tongue is figure only,
Old or young the tongue is lonely.
Yet when either old or young
Twice I sound in Roman tongue.

II.

In the noble's stately hall,
Mid the splendors of the ball,
In the upland hamlets' play,
. On a sunshine holiday,
Rustic maids and courtly dames
Know me by fantastic names :
But the bird upon the spray
Knows me better far than they.

III.

Shepherds slumbering in the lawn
Often are by painters drawn :
Such my picture—yet I doubt
If by that you find me out.
In the lawn is many a fold
Not the peaceful sheep to hold.
Lawn and fold mid war's alarms
Hold the slumbering shepherd's arms.

1. I'm terror to many.
2. Worst ancient of any.
3. Place to lay out a penny.

I. H.

No. 127.

Van and rear guard of the band
Nurtured in a classic land,
Bringing from their native shore
Science, art, and ancient lore.
Seeming, each when in its place,
Sentinels of time and space.
Join them, and we strain our sight
Onward to the infinite.

1. His darts both men and horses slay.
2. Drink, and sleep your cares away.
3. Robe of mountains bleak and cold.
4. For witchcraft burned in days of old.
5. A king to whom the truth was told.

M'C.

No. 128.

I stood before her, but my tongue was tied,
And utterance of my passion was denied:
Dashed and amazed I stood like one accursed,
Haunted by fiends and goblins of my first.

My second tells when **blushed the anxious dame**
How words at **will to suit my passion came.**
I told my love, she did not say me nay.
How my heart beat my modest **whole** will say.

1. The mode to put my question **to** the fair.
2. The land whose **wealth is** worthless in compare
3. **With the small toy** she gave when faith we sware.

I. H.

No. 129.

My whole is my first, **if my second were whole,**
My whole would **be no where and I should be sole.**

1. **Child of** sorrow **and desire,**
   I am born when **you expire.**
2. **With the motions of the deep**
   I have life, and **time I keep.**
3. Still to solve my **secret try,**
   But my name is mystery.
4. **Every failure I declare**
   As you wander here and there.
5. I'll tell what your **success** will be
   If you solve the **mystery.**

I. H.

No. 130.

I.
What's given to me in pence or notes
A fair equivalent denotes.
Bright! is my cry, there's nought like leather,
Reform brings high and low together.

II.
In private box, to child of cit
I'm more than trap-door, stage, and pit,
And in the green, the country child
Makes audience to my antics wild.

III.
Your artist ready stands to draw,
So quiet keep head, trunk and paw,
Just take your ease, and stretch your legs,
For this is all your artist begs.

1. Of Indian towns we don't know much,
   But I'm perhaps the best in Cutch.
2. The provinces are better known,
   I'm near Bengal, and England's own.
3. Light by my nerve the timid find,
   Without it even the brave are blind.
4. And brave and timid owe to me
   The means of mutual colloquy. I. II.

No. 131.

I.
Though for **dinner I've** oft to manœuvre,
Roast meat is alone to my mind.

II.
I am one out of two, **the chef-d'œuvre**
Which **the last of our artists designed.**

III.
The martin **he comes with the summer,**
With the **autumn he passes away**;
I shine on chief, trooper, and drummer,
With the martin I too have my day.

1. I've a charm for the **ins** and the outs.
2. I've a charm for the Bulls **and** the Bears.
3. If I'm bishop I still have my doubts.
4. What **needles** do only in pairs.

I.H.

No. 132.

The force of letters let grammarians tell,
The force of numbers tune the poet's shell:
Mine is the glory which to both is due,
The force of letters and of numbers too.

In Ireland placed near ocean's saddening hues,
Despite Disraeli, I eschew the blues.
The two known names of him who gave me birth
To two-fold street boys grant divided mirth.
They dock the one to deck my English peer,
The other lengthened designates me here,
Who represent in dubious green array
An Irish force derived from English sway.

1. While ebb and flow within my limits be,
   I drown upon the land, but save at sea.
2. Though natural tints should rustic cheek suffuse,
   The clowns I know cosmetics ever use.
3. To every one how soon my name were known,
   Would Lady Lurewell leave but well alone.
4. Miss Languish sought the absolute we know,
   In me she'd find a different kind of beau.

5. Gay Sidney brought perfection **to a pea**,
   Oh! how he'd fly from dreary perfect **me**.
6. Though I've a court, there's very little **doubt**
   That court should **ever strive** to keep me **out**.

I.H.

No. 133.
I.

The **friend I** most **desire** to greet
   Is all a friend should **be**,
And, like my first, whene'er **we meet**,
   Is gentle, kind, and free.
My second, though **not quite so rare**,
   Is soft and peaceful **too** :
On earth, on ocean, **and** in air
   'Tis seldom out of view.
Clad in a gorgeous coat of mail,
   Yet innocent of strife,
My whole comes fluttering on the **gale**,
   A **tiny** speck of life.

1. Blithesome, frisky, playful thing.
2. City of an ancient king.
3. Destined twice to fill a throne.
4. Length I am, and length alone.   M'C.

No. 134.

I.
Child of the waters,
   Fragile and fair,
A garb of the loveliest
   Colours I wear,
I die on the earth, and I live in the air.

II.
In pain, and in pleasure,
   In comfort or cold,
'Tis the voice of a youngster
   That seldom grows old.

III.
On a bed of leaves
   It lowly lies,
To vanish soon
   From longing eyes.

1. Some bitter thoughts my memory brings.
2. The gallic boaster spreads his wings.
3. Lively ladies like me well.
4. Admired I am by every swell.
5. With fiery force I speed my course.
6. No more in Erin's Isle I dwell.   M'C.

No. 135.

I.

My senses varied elements combine,
　　Comprising all within a narrow span,
The waters' flow, or produce of the mine,
　　Or fire, or beast, or eloquence of man.

II.

Here too in equal space the little stage
　　Presents to view a still more varied scene,
For here by turns or democratic rage,
　　Or modest street, or gondolier is seen.

III.

Here lie, when carried to their home at last,
　　The maudlin Saxon, and the Celtic chief;
My labour present, and my duty past
　　To bear oblivion and to bury grief.

1. The first my first repeated.
2. And when you've let the middle
   Make addition in the riddle,
3. Then the whole will quite complete it.

F.

No. 136.

I.

I'm given oft for love, for gain,
 In playful games I'm taken,
Stiff in contention I remain,
 Only in friendship shaken.

II.

I may be many, may be few,
 My numbers great or small,
But still whatever I can do
 I never can be all.

III.

Fair Rosa still with tingling ear,
 Vain of her form and dress,
The pleasant flattery shall hear
 We meet but to express.

1. I am the god of eloquence and gain.
2. And I'm a ship that whilome clove the main.
3. And I a town that gives a county name.
4. And I a bird most loving and most tame.

E.

No. 137.

With piercing steel in eager speed
   As onward still I fly
The long thin wavering line I lead,
   Is ever in mine eye.

Faithful I followed him through all,
   But soon as all was done,
I found myself in captive thrall
   And my keen leader gone.

1. I am not gaudy, and I am not mean.
2. A lion-hearted and an island queen.
3. And I a queen too of religious fame.
4. The consort of a knight has borne my name.
5. I am a great high priest of mystic birth.
6. The Cymric festival makes Saxon mirth.

                              E.

No. 138.

I.

A beauteous name, once borne by her confest
Of womanhood the holiest, purest, best.
By her whose wondrous beauty, sin, and sorrow,
A passing tribute from our tears may borrow.

II.

For me the sailor strives, the soldier bleeds,
For me the lawyer frames his words and deeds,
For me the Irish peasant craves and cries,
For me the farmer lives, the patriot dies.

III.

A fraction of a once united whole,
I sought the cause of freedom to control,
Yet, when from persecution forced to flee
The wanderers found a peaceful home in me.

1. To merit I'm given.
2. For freedom I've striven.
3. In measure a treasure.
4. A treasure to measure.

M. P.

No. 139.

Unlike in structure, sense, and sound,
No common letter to be found,
   Yet might I pledge my troth,
Such curious words compose my theme,
That, when you name my first, you seem
   Perforce to mention both.
My second's sure to come as well,
Possessing a familiar spell
   For soothing as for teasing.
For once refreshing, cool and nice,
Yet, if you chance to say it twice,
   It is not half so pleasing.
My whole recalls a fatal fight,
A lovely dame, and felon knight.

1. Most famous of fields, but for me and my men,
   Old Europe enfranchised were perilled again.
2. What standards were rent in that fearful affray;
   And I, the most famous of standards, away!
3. You all know my pencil, of pencils the sharpest.
4. A royal, a Celtic, magnificent harpist.

                                                    O.

No. 140.

Where'er I go,
As all men know,
I beat my hapless wife.
Though smiles I bring,
And laughs that ring,
I cut as with a knife.

A man of jest,
I've done my best
All Englishmen to please;
I'm cut in twain,
And cut again,
And often get a squeeze.

1. My normal state
   Is tumult great.
2. For me alone
   No equal's known.
3. To strangers I
   Will nothing give.
4. In rhyme, deny
   It not, I live.
5. Though I unite
   I sever quite.

L..

No. 141.

I.

A loyal race from days of old,
Gentle in peace, in warfare bold,
Science and art our works disclose
Before the tower of Babel rose.

II.

And yet without my second, all
Our glories fade, our fabrics fall,
Our spirit dies, the earthly crust
Descends, and mingles with the dust.

III.

Seen darkly through a glass my whole
For joys to come prepares the soul,
And deans who sixty-eight deplore,
For me would double thirty-four.

1. Soft and gentle, cooling too ;
   Hot and heavy, black and blue.
2. A father and a priest defied—
   The children slain, the priest and father died.

3. There father **Thames** with pride surveys
   Old **England**'s sons in early **days**.
4. Of stately and majestic mien,
   He falls before a foe unseen.

M'C.

No. 142.

A daughter of Erin I sued,
  She was fair as fair could be,
And I asked her as well as I could
  If the fair one mine would be.
Said she "my first have you got?"
  Don't smile, 'tis not to be reckoned
More real than money, I wot;
  Said I, " No;" "Then are you my second?"
"'Tis that second, my fair," said I,
  "That I fain would be to you,
But I own that I'm not so high
  As yet, if I tell you true."
Said the fair one "without my first
  You never could be my whole."
I saw things were come to the worst,
  And was vexed to my very soul,

So I turned my face to the door,
And, after a little pause,
I'm afraid that I almost swore,
Swore " **I'd** be shot if I was."

1. **A** pause when stormy tempests blow.
2. **A** fuss with much less work than show.
3. **In all events I'm** kept below.
4. Is there assurance greater? No.

I. H.

No. 143.

Then the daughter of **Erin rose**,
   A sweet **Celt** nose upturning,
And I felt from **my** head **to my toes**,
   The fire in the grey eyes burning.
' When you come to see what you have botched
   Your blood may be sometimes spilt, sir,
But when with your stewards we're scotched,
   No wonder that you should be kilt, sir !"

1. My trembling tones divinely falter
   Twixt Donizetti and Sir Walter.
2. Snowy white, and ritualistic—
   (Friends will please accept this distich).

3. On **Shelley's** pinnace fortune frowned—
   I'm shelly, too, but never drowned.
4. Like **pistols**, dangerous when loaded,
   'Twere **safer** far were both exploded.
5. Spirits who human touch eschew,
   Nor waste their time on mountain dew.
6. In opposition colors dight.
   " I thank thee Jew,"—an obvious light !
7. Kisses sweet neath mistletoe,
   Under me more sweetly grow.
8. Marmalade, and Killiecrankie,
   Both are mine—I'm finished, thank'ee.

O'L..

No. 144.

This is the last of all my doubles,
  And when 'tis ended, I vow and swear
I'll blow no more of these colored bubbles
  That float a moment to melt in air.
They're death and ruin to all my reading,
  The charms of prose and the heights of song,
As I count on my fingers the words succeeding
  To try if the letters go right or wrong.

So this is my last; and my first will bring you
    Back half a thousand years of time,
And summon an elder bard to sing you,
    In strains as fresh as the May morn prime,
How the good knight's sword lay at rest in scabbard,
    And the laughing dame rode abroad to pray,
And those nine and twenty met at the Tabard
    With one who has made them survive for aye.

My next is full of the busy present,
    And fuller still of the days to be,
Of an onward march, and a rush incessant
    To a goal predestined to fade and flee,
Of science, queen of a mighty era,—
    Of hope unfolding the future's plan;
But alas! of many a fond chimæra,
    For ever and ever denied to man.

Times and feelings so wide asunder,
    Where is the power that shall blend in one!
Genius and faith may achieve the wonder,
    And lo! the task is already done.
Behold the hero, though wiles ensnare him,
    Though foes encircle, and pitfalls yawn,
Valour and hope at the last will bear him,
    To the golden gates, and the realm of dawn.

1. Words however soft they be
   Seek in vain to soften me.
2. White the plain, and dark my stream,
   'Tis a glorious lyric theme.
3. Vain is struggling, vain is flying
   From the noose there's no untying!
4. Vanquished by the fatal wood,
   Open-mouthed and mute he stood!
5. Pausing from the goal that's near,
   Wandering for my partner dear.
6. Pity us, unhappy twain
   Called so often to explain.
7. What displeasure at the making,
   What enjoyment in partaking.
8. "Stop us!" what an awful threat
   Seldom executed yet.

O.

"Οὐράνιαι νεφέλαι, μεγάλαι θεάι ἀνδράσιν ἀργοῖς."

www.ingramcontent.com/pod-product-compliance
Lightning Source LLC
Chambersburg PA
CBHW030308170426
43202CB00009B/915